Orca
Origins

Jen Sookfong Lee

CHINESE NEW YEAR

A Celebration for Everyone

ORCA BOOK PUBLISHERS

Text copyright © Jen Sookfong Lee 2017, 2021

Published in Canada and the United States in 2021 by Orca Book Publishers.
Previously published in 2017 by Orca Book Publishers as a hardcover (ISBN 9781459811263).
orcabook.com

Library and Archives Canada Cataloguing in Publication
Title: Chinese New Year: a celebration for everyone / Jen Sookfong Lee.
Names: Lee, Jen Sookfong, author.
Series: Orca origins.
Description: Series statement: Orca origins | Previously published: 2017. |
Includes bibliographical references and index.
Identifiers: Canadiana 20200232819 | ISBN 9781459826434 (softcover)
Subjects: LCSH: Chinese New Year—Juvenile literature.
Classification: LCC GT4905 .L44 2021 | DDC j394.261—dc23

Library of Congress Control Number: 2020931820

Summary: Part of the nonfiction Orca Origins series, Chinese New Year is illustrated with color photographs
throughout. Readers will learn how a simple gathering of family and friends grew into a weeklong, worldwide festival.

Orca Book Publishers is committed to reducing the consumption of non-renewable resources in the
making of our books. We make every effort to use materials that support a sustainable future.

Orca Book Publishers gratefully acknowledges the support for its publishing programs provided by
the following agencies: the Government of Canada, the Canada Council for the Arts and the Province
of British Columbia through the BC Arts Council and the Book Publishing Tax Credit.

Edited by Sarah N. Harvey
Designed by Rachel Page
Front cover photos by yupiyan/iStock.com, Toa55/iStock.com,
somethingway/iStock.com and THEGIFT777/iStock.com
Back cover photo by aluxum/iStock.com
Author photo by Kyrani Kanavaros

Printed and bound in South Korea.

24 23 22 21 • 1 2 3 4

For my nieces and nephews: Nicholas, Madeleine, Joshua, Caitlyn, Benjamin and Lauren.
And especially for my son, Oscar.

CONTENTS

Chapter Four:
Chinese New Year Celebrations Across the Globe

Lion dances are often performed during Chinese New Year but also during other celebrations, such as weddings or new business openings.
aluxum/iStock.com

A Chinese New Year parade in Victoria, BC, where many Chinese immigrants to Canada first disembarked in the late 19th and early 20th centuries.
Robert Amos

INTRODUCTION

When I was a little girl, I lived with my parents, my grandparents and my four older sisters. I grew up in Vancouver, British Columbia, which is home to a large Chinese Canadian community and one of the oldest Chinatowns in North America. My grandfather came to Canada in 1913 at the age of 17 and eventually became a barber. For many years he owned the only barbershop in Chinatown. He lived in an apartment around the corner from the shop, ate his meals at the Hong Kong Café on Pender Street, and stopped at the newsstand every morning to buy papers in English and Chinese. At that time, he was one of a handful of Chinese men who could read both languages and often helped others with reading and writing letters, or filling out government forms.

My grandfather in the 1960s, after my grand-mother, father and mother joined him in Canada. This photograph was taken in our first family home in East Vancouver.

Jen Sookfong Lee

Dragons are often printed on calendars and lucky money envelopes. Stone dragons are used to decorate buildings, particularly in pairs at entrances. And brides will often wear a **cheongsam** (a Chinese-style silk dress) embroidered with twisting dragons.

My family, including my grandparents, in 1978.
Jen Sookfong Lee

For my sisters and me, who were born in Canada, Chinatown felt like home. We knew every restaurant, bakery and grocery store. On the days we didn't have school, our grandfather would take us to his favorite diner and buy us apple tarts while he had a cup of coffee and a doughnut. Our mother haggled with the shop owners she saw twice a week, looking for the leanest piece of roasted pork belly or the best price on pomelos, a giant citrus fruit the size of a volleyball. When we were sick, we drank the soup the traditional Chinese doctor prepared from dried roots, berries and herbs. If we drank the sometimes very bitter soup without complaining, the doctor would reward us with a roll of Haw Flakes, a type of Chinese candy that was round, flat and slightly chewy.

At the end of every winter, in late January or early February, our father took us to watch the Chinese New Year

parade, which snaked through Chinatown on New Year's Day. My mother usually stayed home to prepare the New Year's Day meal, an eight-course dinner that took her days to plan. In the damp cold, we watched the dancers, drummers and martial arts performers march and spin, while firecrackers filled the air with noise and smoke. Our cousins Tony and Sonny were often part of the team of teenage boys who formed the body of the dancing dragon, which was made of silk and held up with long wooden poles. Local politicians and other dignitaries marching in the parade passed out candy to all the children, and we called out "**Gung hay fat choy**," the traditional New Year greeting that wishes prosperity or wealth for the year ahead.

Our faces pink with cold, we piled back into the car and drove home, ready to start eating the sweet and savory

My family when I was a little girl in 1983.
Jen Sookfong Lee

Chinese New Year parades, like this one, are popular with people from all different cultures.
Robert Amos

dumplings my mother had started frying that morning. There would be crispy shrimp chips, sticky date cake and steamed cupcakes that looked like tulips. And after that, the big event—a celebratory dinner at which our parents and uncles and aunts would trade happy stories and good wishes long into the night. We ate prawns, noodles, soup, steamed fish, mushrooms and piles of greens, all cooked by my mother. For dessert, we ate fresh fruit and more candy than we were ever allowed to eat the rest of the year.

Chinese people live in many cities throughout the world, and Chinese New Year celebrations are a little bit different everywhere you go. But my family, like most other Chinese families in every part of the world, always rings in the New Year with our loved ones, good food, and lots and lots of laughter. Today, now that I'm a mother, I love following the same traditions with my son: going to the Chinese New Year parade, teaching him about the different customs and foods, and using that time to talk with our extended family, especially my mother. She still cooks us a huge dinner and greets every single one of her grandchildren with a kiss and a piece of candy. Chinese New Year is always fun, but it's important for me to teach my son that the celebrations are a snapshot of Chinese culture. Every food item means something. The **Chinese zodiac** and its twelve animal signs mean something. The red envelopes of lucky money (called **lai see** in Chinese) we give and receive is more than just money. This is also why I'm writing this book. Chinese New Year is a popular and well-known holiday, but like Christmas or Halloween, it grew out of history and stories. To understand Chinese New Year is to understand what makes Chinese culture unique. And I want all of you to celebrate your next Chinese New Year with a deeper understanding of what the dragons and firecrackers really, truly mean. So keep reading!

In the 1950s, '60s and '70s, when immigration to Canada and the United States was very high, Chinatowns across North America were especially busy, with families shopping for groceries, tourists looking for souvenirs like porcelain Buddhas and lacquered chopsticks, and young people hoping to hear live music.

What Kids Say About Chinese New Year

I asked the children in my life, all of whom are members of Chinese Canadian families, to tell me their favorite parts of the celebrations. Here's what they said.

"Money! And seeing all our grandmas and grandpas. And sitting in our uncle's massage chair!"

—Samuel (age 9) and Lea (age 6)

"The party! And eating with the family."

—Maya (age 7)

"Being with all the family, and playing and stuff."

—Sebastien (age 9)

"The parade! Because of the dragon thing. I like the big mouth!"

—Oscar (age 6)

During Chinese New Year, lanterns in the shape of the coming year's zodiac animal are one of the most popular decorations.

kristyewing/iStock.com

WHAT CHINESE NEW YEAR IS ALL ABOUT

Mythic Origins

Chinese New Year, also known as the **Lunar New Year** or the **Spring Festival**, is the biggest holiday in China, in many other countries in Asia, and for the communities of Chinese people who live all over the world. There is gift-giving, lots of food, and visiting with family and friends. The celebrations often last for one or two weeks, so it's a lot like the winter holidays of Christmas, Hanukkah and New Year's Eve all rolled into one. And its origins, like those of Christmas and Hanukkah, are thousands of years old.

Chinese New Year has been celebrated for so long that no one knows exactly when it began, although some

Drumming is prominent during Chinese New Year, both to scare off evil spirits and to provide accompaniment to the lion dancers.
aluxum/iStock.com

historians guess that it began as a holiday around 2000 BCE. According to legend, a mythical beast or monster known as the **Nián**, which is also the Chinese word for "year," appeared before the coming of spring, bringing illness and bad luck to families still struggling to survive a long, cold winter. An old man advises villagers to scare the Nián away with the color red, bright lights and loud noises. So, in the night, the people wore red clothing, hung red banners and paper cut-outs in doorways and windows, and lit firecrackers. And it worked! The Nián retreated, and every year on that same day, people in China celebrate this victory over the Nián, but also over the hardships of winter. In the morning, it was a brand-new day, and people were ready to begin their preparations for spring and the year's crops.

Thean Hou Buddhist temple decorated in red for the New Year.
CollinsChin/iStock.com

Jade Emperor statue.
nbriam/iStock.com

Another legend features the powerful **Jade Emperor**. In Chinese mythology, the Jade Emperor was in charge of a godly court and oversaw the other gods who were in charge of their own domains, like Tian Hou, who governed the sea and protected fishermen, or the Kitchen Gods, who took care of villages and families. In some Chinese houses, families install a **shrine** to the Kitchen God of their home village, which is usually an open-sided red box with a porcelain figure of that god. During the week and especially on important dates such as holidays or birthdays, the family will place fruit, tea and incense in the box as an offering. Keeping the god happy is believed to help the family's fortunes.

One day, the Jade Emperor grew frustrated with how to measure the passage of time. He decided to create a calendar and to name each year after an animal. He held a race across a wide river, and the first year would be named

CNY Facts

In Chinese culture, numbers and how they're used are very important and are often believed to influence someone's luck. During the New Year celebrations, this belief, called *numerology*, is especially important.

In our family, my mother always prepared an even number of dishes for our big dinner—either eight or ten, but never an odd number. Red lucky envelopes were given away in pairs.

Traditionally, the luckiest number is eight, because, when spoken in Chinese, it can sound like the word for "wealth." The number six is also considered lucky because it sounds similar to the word for "smooth" or "well-off." And there is one number to avoid, and that number is four, which can sound like the word for "death." In Hong Kong, public auctions are held to sell the luckiest license plate numbers. When planning big events, like weddings, graduations or the opening of a business, calendars are carefully consulted to make sure the date is a good number. And in Vancouver, which has a large Asian population, high-rise buildings are often missing floors four, fourteen and twenty-four.

RAT　OX　TIGER　RABBIT

DRAGON　SNAKE　HORSE　GOAT

MONKEY　ROOSTER　DOG　PIG

The twelve animals of the Chinese lunar calendar.
anttohoho/iStock.com

for the first animal to cross the finish line. The first was the clever Rat, followed by eleven other animals, each with their own strengths and weaknesses that contributed to how quickly or slowly they completed the race. That is why the Chinese calendar, or **lunar calendar**, is split into twelve-year cycles, with each year named after one of the twelve animals. At the end of the Jade Emperor's race, he held a great celebration for the first day of the New Year, the year of the Rat.

You may have noticed that Chinese New Year isn't on the same day every year. That's because holidays usually follow the lunar calendar, which follows the phases of the moon (the Latin word for "moon" is *luna*). The traditional Chinese month begins with the new moon, invisible in the night sky, and the days follow the moon as it waxes, or grows bigger. The full moon, in the middle of the month, then begins to wane, or grow smaller, until it disappears, marking a new moon and a new month.

Chinese New Year is celebrated at the beginning of the second month after the winter solstice, or the shortest day of the year. It marks the end of winter as well as the beginning of spring and the start of a brand-new year. Each year in the lunar calendar is represented by an animal. The Rat, of course, is the first, and the other eleven are the Ox, Tiger, Rabbit, Dragon, Snake, Horse, Goat, Monkey, Rooster, Dog and Pig. Each of these animals has specific traits. For example, the Monkey is mischievous and the Rooster is proud. People born in those years are said to have these same traits. All together, these animals and years make up the Chinese zodiac, which works much the same way as the Western zodiac: your date of birth determines what kind of person you're likely to be.

Every year during Chinese New Year celebrations, the coming year's zodiac animal is paid special attention, with calendars, paper cut-outs and stuffed toys. In 2016, the year of the Monkey, the Taipei Zoo in Taiwan prepared for extra visitors to its twenty-five species of primates, including chimpanzees, orangutans and lemurs. And monkey pajamas, cufflinks and purses were all available for sale.

The Not-So-Mythic Story

For centuries, most of the people who lived in China were farmers who rented their farms from wealthy landowners. Usually, these landowners would collect the rent owed them on the last day of the year—New Year's Eve. This, of course, was a day that filled farmers with dread.

CNY Facts

Just for fun, take a look at the following list to see if the animal sign you were born under sounds like you.

Rat: 1984, 1996, 2008, 2020
Clever, charming, ambitious

Ox: 1985, 1997, 2009, 2021
Determined, patient, honest

Tiger: 1986, 1998, 2010
Brave, strong, daring

Rabbit: 1987, 1999, 2011
Caring, creative, peaceful

Dragon: 1988, 2000, 2012
Powerful, lucky, wise

Snake: 1989, 2001, 2013
Calm, intelligent, elegant

Horse: 1990, 2002, 2014
Popular, independent, clever

Goat: 1991, 2003, 2015
Artistic, sensitive, caring

Monkey: 1992, 2004, 2016
Mischievous, confident, inventive

Rooster: 1993, 2005, 2017
Adventurous, kind, proud

Dog: 1994, 2006, 2018
Loyal, loving, intelligent

Pig: 1995, 2007, 2019
Noble, peaceful, forgiving

Sometimes the harvest hadn't been plentiful, and the farmers hadn't saved enough money. Sometimes the landowners would raise the rent without notice. Surviving this day was a goal for many families.

The next day, the first day of the New Year, was often celebrated with a grand feast, loud fireworks and games of **Mahjong** (the popular Chinese tile game that is sometimes compared to poker). My grandmother and mother were dedicated Mahjong players, and both had a large circle of friends with whom they organized games that lasted long into the night. For many Chinese women who moved to Canada or other countries, Mahjong tournaments became an essential way for them to meet other women and make friends. Most of these women were stay-at-home wives and mothers and therefore didn't socialize at workplaces, as their husbands did. So, in organizing Mahjong parties, they got to know one

Mahjong, the popular Chinese tile game, is played all over the world.
real444/iStock.com

another, developed lifelong friendships and celebrated the end of another bleak winter, which was always cause for great joy! As Chinese communities grew around the world, these home celebrations eventually became the elaborate Chinese New Year festivals.

These mythic and non-mythic stories are the basis for how Chinese people around the world celebrate the New Year today. People still dress in red and light firecrackers, and in many countries you will see red and gold banners hanging in shop windows. Often one of the twelve calendar animals—such as the Dragon, Pig or Monkey—is on these banners. Like many different holidays from other cultures, Chinese New Year honors tradition and the old stories passed down from generation to generation.

Firecrackers are used on Chinese New Year to scare away bad luck.
MonicaNinker/iStock.com

CNY Facts

During Chinese New Year, people pay close attention to the words they use in order to attract good luck for the coming year. This can be tricky in Chinese, which has a lot of *homophones*, or words that sound the same but have different meanings, like the English words "hear" and "here." We've already discussed how the number four can sound like the word for "death." *Fat choy*, the black moss that is commonly used in a soup made especially during the New Year celebrations, sounds a lot like the word for "prosperity" and is part of the very common New Year greeting "Gung hay fat choy." The Chinese word for "lettuce" sounds very much like the word for "making money," which is why my mother always prepared a dish for our New Year dinner with braised shiitake mushrooms and leaves of iceberg lettuce. Sometimes, when people who are new to Chinese are learning the language, making sense of all the homophones can be difficult. Chinese speakers have fun by using puns in jokes and comedy shows. The Chinese language has only 400 syllable sounds, which seems like a lot, but English contains more than 15,000! That means many Chinese words sound the same, adding to the confusion, but also to the fun.

How Chinese New Year Changed

Chinese New Year usually falls between January 21 and February 19 and began as a public celebration in the fourteenth century. Until 1912, China was under imperial rule, meaning it was governed by emperors and empresses who inherited their roles through their families, very much like the kings and queens of other countries, such as England. After 1912, China became a **republic**, or a country governed by a constitution, a document that describes how the country is to be run and what rights and freedoms citizens have. At the time, the government wanted China to become more Western and to appear more modern, so it began calling the New Year celebrations the Spring

The emperor Qianlong.
windmoon/Shutterstock.com

Spring Festival family dinner in Sichuan Province.
pengyou91/iStock.com

Festival instead, hoping that the people of China would start honoring the Western New Year.

However, many world events that occurred in the years that followed affected Chinese citizens in everyday ways, including how and when they celebrated holidays. World War II and the Communist Party, which still governs China today, were especially important to the country's history. There were many years, even up until the 1980s, when villages and cities didn't mark the holiday at all. Many ordinary Chinese families were poor, and the government was still trying to build up the country after the devastating destruction of World War II.

That war, which lasted in China from 1937 to 1945, is still a painful memory for many Chinese people. The war was fought in many countries of Europe and is most remembered as a long-running conflict between Nazi Germany and the allied countries of Great Britain and France. But it was

"There was a lot of storytelling going on in our house: family stories, gossip, what happened to the people left behind in China."
—*Amy Tan, author*

21

A World War II tank displayed in Tianjin, China.
pkujiahe/iStock.com

also fought in Asia, where Japan battled to gain control of other Asian countries, including China. Japanese forces entered, fought in and occupied much of China, including big cities like Shanghai. As many as twenty million Chinese people died during the years of fighting. In 1945, Japan was defeated, and China began the long process of rebuilding its cities and towns.

By the 1980s and '90s, China was loosening its strict rules on businesses. Its citizens had more money than ever before, and they wanted to celebrate their good fortune! So the Spring Festival, as it's still called, became the biggest annual holiday in China and in Chinese communities around the world. It became so big that the Chinese government officially made it a weeklong national holiday, a time when people can take time off work, rest and enjoy themselves.

When Politics and Holidays Collide

Whenever we talk about the history of Chinese New Year, it's important to talk about politics. China has been through a lot in the twentieth and twenty-first centuries. The government has undergone many changes, and this has had a direct impact on the celebrations during Chinese New Year.

During and after World War II, families in China were struggling to survive after years of violence that left the country in ruins. Two political groups, the Communist Party and the Kuomintang (also known as the Nationalist Party of China) were fighting each other, trying to gain control of the government. It was very disorganized after the war. Eventually, in 1949, the Communist Party formed

A military exercise held in Beijing, China, to recognize the 70th Anniversary of the end of World War II.
lufengkll/iStock.com

the People's Republic of China, which China is still officially known as today. Until the 1980s, the Communist
Party enforced very strict laws for the country's citizens,
including the famous one-child policy that limited families to having only one child. At that time, China's population was growing quickly. The government, worried about
producing enough food and having to build more homes,
wanted to slow that growth down. In 1958, China's then-
leader, Chairman **Mao Zedong** (sometimes also known as
Mao Tse Tung), started a program which was called the
Great Leap Forward, designed to help China move quickly
into manufacturing and away from farming. People were
forced to live and work in communes or camps. Farms
were bulldozed for the building of factories, making food
scarce. No one knows for sure how many people died
because of starvation or forced labor during the four

Mao Zedong pictured on Chinese currency.
Yestock/iStock.com

哲学
哲学

years of the Great Leap Forward, but the number could be anywhere from eighteen to forty-five million.

In order to recover from the devastation caused by the Great Leap Forward, the government then created several new programs across the country to make sure everyone had enough food to eat. While this helped end the famine, it also angered Chairman Mao. Because the Great Leap Forward had been his idea, he saw its failure as an attack on him personally. He felt betrayed by the government's decision to end the Great Leap Forward. In 1966, he began a movement called the Cultural Revolution, which was meant to take down the government he had built. During the revolution, several million more people who had opposed Mao's decisions died from violence, often because of the Red Guards, an army made up of ordinary young people, some as young as 15 or 16 years old. They were encouraged to oppose their local leaders and were responsible for much of the violence that lasted until 1976.

Poster of the Red Guards in China in the 1970s.
John Lock/Shutterstock.com

Have you ever seen a label on a toy or a shirt that says "Made in China"? Manufacturing, or the making of things that can be sold and bought, is the backbone of China's recent success. Some products you may not know were made in China are shoes, cement, light bulbs and air conditioners.

Poster from the Cultural Revolution.
John Lock/Shutterstock.com

Although Mao Zedong is talked about in other parts of the world as a **dictator** (a government leader who doesn't listen to the people or his advisors) his reputation within China is still mostly positive. Because the Communist Party has been in government since 1949, it controls the information about Mao and his policies. In fact, Chairman Mao's government produced many posters, songs, books and plays that carried a hidden message: that the Communist Party and Mao Zedong were doing a great job of governing China. This was one of the many ways Chairman Mao kept control over a huge country and hundreds of millions of people. Much of what we know about him is still censored in China, where he is seen as the father of modern China.

During the Great Leap Forward and the Cultural Revolution, Chinese New Year was hardly celebrated at all. Chinese citizens had little or no spending money, and many families were simply concerned with trying to survive. Celebrating any holiday just wasn't a priority. However, in the 1980s, when China began to encourage people to start and build businesses, many people started making and spending more money. New Year celebrations began to grow. Now China is one the richest and most powerful countries in the world, and the Spring Festival is an elaborate and extravagant holiday.

However, the Chinese government continued to make headlines for the way it treats its citizens, particularly those who have spoken out about human rights or democracy. In 1989, the military violently shut down protests that university students had organized, including a famous one in Tiananmen Square in Beijing. Thousands of protestors died there. Now organizations are protesting on behalf of the people who work in the many factories throughout

"I was fortunate enough to have a mother who could put together multiple courses for a Chinese meal on a daily basis without any recipes or training."
—Judy Chan, cooking teacher

Tiananmen Gate in Beijing, China.
Leonid Andronov/iStock.com

School children preparing for the Chinese New Year parade outside the Victoria Chinese Public School in Victoria, BC.
Robert Amos

China that manufacture items such as smartphones, toys and clothing. During the New Year holiday, these underpaid workers, who usually live in dormitory-style buildings owned by the factories, cannot afford to travel to their home cities to visit their families. And so, during the Spring Festival, demonstrations are often organized, and protestors get arrested. In a country that has experienced and continues to experience so much turmoil, inevitably the year's biggest holiday is affected.

Chinese School and the New Year

Like many children from Chinese families living in North America, I attended Chinese language school on Saturday mornings until I was 13. Our parents, who mostly spoke Chinese at home, were worried that we would grow up speaking only English, so language lessons were very important to them. We learned to read, write and speak Cantonese, a common dialect many Chinese people speak.

Chinese New Year was very important in these classes. Teaching us about the traditions and stories was a way to make learning fun. We cooked **tay**, the special sweet and salty snacks, often dumplings, and performed songs in a

New Year concert for our families. Our teachers brought in special brushes and bottles of ink so we could try making our own banners with **calligraphy**, a type of writing that is similar to painting, just like the villagers did when they scared away the Nián. The best part for me was when the entire school gathered around the head teacher, and she told us the stories of the Nián and the twelve racing animals.

As I'm sure you can imagine, going to school on Saturday was not my favorite thing to do, but I understand now that it was important for me to participate in the culture my parents and grandparents came from. My son has just recently said he would like to learn Chinese, so it seems that the tradition of going to school on the weekend will be passed on to at least one more generation.

Sesame peanut brittle.
Dolly MJ/Shutterstock.com

When making this recipe as well as the other recipes in this book, be sure an adult is around to supervise.

Sesame Peanut Brittle

During Chinese New Year, people eat a lot of candy and other sweets—enthusiastically! My mother always told me that eating sweet things would help ensure that the coming year would be just as sweet. Many Chinese candies are difficult to make, and require lots of steps and ingredients, but below is a simple brittle recipe with some key Asian flavors. Cane sugar is a type of brown sugar that has been formed into hard cakes that must be broken up or ground before it can be used. It is available at Asian grocery stores.

Ingredients:

⅛ cup vegetable oil
(for brushing the pan)

2 cups shelled roasted peanuts
(or any other nut you like)

⅓ cup sesame seeds

1 cup cane sugar or brown sugar

½ teaspoon ground ginger

½ teaspoon cinnamon

¼ teaspoon ground star anise

Directions:

1. Line a cookie sheet with parchment paper and brush with the oil.
2. Spread peanuts and sesame seeds evenly on the cookie sheet.
3. Break the cane sugar into pieces and place them in a saucepan with the ginger, cinnamon and star anise. Heat over medium-high heat until the sugar has melted, about 5 minutes.
4. Pour the sugar mixture over the nuts and spread evenly on the cookie sheet with a heat-proof spatula.
5. Let the mixture cool until it hardens, about 20 minutes. Break the brittle into bite-sized pieces.

Janie's Story

Janie Chang.
[stu-di-o] by Jeanie

When author Janie Chang was a child in the 1970s in Vancouver, her family always got together with the same group of families to celebrate holidays. The biggest celebration of all was Chinese New Year. For the grown-ups, the highlight was a huge **potluck** buffet dinner. Janie's mother, along with the other women, each brought not one, but several platters of food to contribute to this meal! Since there was no discussion in advance, sometimes there might be red-cooked beef stew from three different kitchens, or five kinds of steamed dumplings or multiple bowls of almond tofu pudding.

For Janie and the other kids, food was not the main attraction. They quickly loaded up their plates, gobbled down their meals and then headed down the basement stairs to the two Mahjong tables their mothers had abandoned. It was now time for a raucous game of Twenty One.

They piled the Mahjong tiles into their boxes and cleared the tables. From somewhere, decks of cards and a bag of roasted watermelon seeds appeared. Although they had all received red envelopes of New Year's cash, the children were absolutely not allowed to bet with real money because that was gambling. Back then, they also couldn't use plastic chips. So they used watermelon seeds, which never lessened the thrill of the game.

Engrossed in playing, some of the kids would nibble away absent-mindedly before realizing they had eaten all their watermelon seeds; then they'd have to give up their place to a new player. If someone lost during a round, that person also had to give up his or her place. It was a noisy game, and Janie and her friends played quickly to get in enough rounds so that everyone could have at least one turn before the women came back. Slow players were jostled along with cries of "Do you want a card or not?"

Then, hearing laughter and conversation as their mothers came down the basement stairs, the children brushed watermelon shells off the white tablecloths and hurriedly put the Mahjong tiles back on the tables. Some of the kids ran upstairs to begin some new game. Some stayed and stood behind their mothers to watch them play. Janie and the others watched the women's chapped hands reach for the middle of the table to mix up the tiles. They watched bejeweled fingers, normally bare of all but plain wedding rings, select tiles to start the first game. And the children watched their mothers carefully count out the watermelon seeds they would use to place their bets.

Mahjong tiles.
pengpeng/iStock.com

Janie Chang in 1968, with her brothers.
Jen Sookfong Lee

Chinatown in San Francisco.
zodebala/iStock.com

TWO

HOW CHINESE NEW YEAR SPREAD AROUND THE WORLD

A Global Community

Over fifty million people with Chinese family history live in countries other than China. Many of them live in other Asian countries such as Singapore or the Philippines, which often hold elaborate Lunar New Year celebrations every year as well. There are large Chinese communities in other parts of the world also, including Australia, Trinidad, the United States and Canada. Some of these communities are hundreds of years old.

There are a few reasons why Chinese people have moved to so many different countries. In the nineteenth century, when China was still struggling with poverty in many of its small villages, people moved to places where

Child doing the lion dance in Bangkok, Thailand.
aluxum/iStock.com

The Confucius Temple in Nanjing City, Jiangsu Province, China.

they could find work. Then they sent the money they earned back to their families in China. The commitment to family, especially the elder members like parents and grandparents, is a philosophy called *filial piety*. Developed by the influential philosopher **Confucius** thousands of years ago, filial piety is the reason Chinese children are expected to show respect and affection for their elders during the New Year, and why people travel to their home cities during festival time. Also, it is part of the reason Chinese people kept looking for better jobs in other countries while their families remained in China. In Chinese culture, it's very important to make life better for your family. China has weathered many changes that have affected everything from food to safety. It makes sense, then, that Chinese families care so much that their home life remains stable. It is the one thing they can rely on.

In the 1960s and '70s, many Chinese people left China to escape the strict Communist government. And, more recently, people have traveled from China to conduct business in other countries. The result? The Chinese communities all over the world are healthy, growing and always changing. The Lunar New Year is always a big party!

My great-grandfather came to Canada in the 1890s, and my grandfather followed in 1913. Back then, the Chinese people who traveled to other countries to live and work were mostly young men. They were the ones who did work like building railways, mining and canning fish. Their families—parents, wives and children—often stayed in China. This meant that these men felt homesick and looked for ways to bring familiar culture and traditions into their lives. My great-grandfather eventually returned

"I'm proud of where I come from: it's between two worlds, and although there are a lot of compromises to make, the margins of two cultures is a very interesting place to be."
—Paul Yee, author

Children participating in a Chinese New Year parade in Vancouver, BC.
Sergei Bachlakov/Shutterstock.com

Many of the Chinese clan associations constructed their own buildings for meetings and events, and they also included small, single-room apartments on the upper floors for new arrivals who hadn't yet found jobs or homes. Now, Chinese seniors occupy these apartments.

City of Vancouver Archives/ COV-S511---:CVA 780-456

"I feel my parents are a part of Canadian history. I feel that they're pioneers. People like my parents who did all the little things are just as important as the story of Canada."
—*Judy Fong Bates, author*

to China and raised his family in his home village. But my grandfather, who was just 17 when he arrived in Vancouver, decided to stay. However, he lived alone in Vancouver until 1951, visiting China every two or three years to see his wife (my grandmother) and their children.

In their new countries, the Chinese formed clan associations, which were groups based on common last names such as Wong, Lee or Chang. They assisted with housing, jobs and learning new languages, and organized events so the men could meet new people and form friendships. My grandfather joined the Lee Association in Vancouver when he arrived and served on its board for years, welcoming new members and guiding them through the immigration process and its confusing paperwork. These associations, and the bonds that formed in every Chinatown, encouraged Chinese immigrants to continue with traditions like Chinese New Year. Later, when I graduated from high school and was preparing to go to university, the Lee Association awarded me a scholarship that helped pay for my tuition. Many clan association buildings in cities such as San Francisco have been renovated to provide housing for Chinese seniors who don't have enough money to rent more expensive apartments and who want to live in a neighborhood that is familiar and comforting. To this day, these organizations are still providing services for their changing communities.

In some countries, Chinese immigrants faced racism, both from governments and people from other cultures. In Canada, for example, Chinese immigrants were not allowed to become citizens and were forced to pay a fee called a **head tax** to enter Canada, a fee that was not imposed on people from other countries. In Trinidad, Chinese men were brought in to work as **indentured laborers** on sugar plantations. Indentured laborers were workers who had agreed to work without pay for years in exchange for the travel costs to get to a new country. They were often treated very poorly by their employers.

CNY Facts

The oldest, largest and most famous Chinatown in North America is in San Francisco. It takes up twelve square blocks and was where the Chinese gold miners who came to California in the 1850s and '60s migrated to when the gold rush was over. In 1906, a devastating earthquake and fire destroyed much of San Francisco and Chinatown. When it came time to rebuild, many of the local Chinese businessmen decided to erect buildings with colorful Asian-style details like rooftop *pagodas* and dragon statues. The Chinese community understood that Chinatown attracted many tourists and wanted the new construction, along with Chinese New Year celebrations, to help bring even more visitors to the neighborhood.

Chinatown in San Francisco.
Ekaterina Pokrovsky/Shutterstock.com

Because of the head tax and other policies, my grandfather lived apart from his family for thirty-eight years. He was one of the first Chinese Canadian men to apply to become a citizen. He received his official citizenship documents in 1949, which allowed him to then bring my grandmother, my father and my two aunts to Canada. It had been his dream all along for his family to become established here, in a country that he considered to be full of possibilities.

My grandfather paid a $500 head tax in 1913, equal to about two years' salary in China. Like most young men, he borrowed the money for the tax and the boat passage from the local council in his home village in China, and spent years paying off the loan in installments. Later, after my grandfather had paid off his debt, he continued to send money to his wife and children. They, in turn, built a new

A head tax certificate from 1922.
Library and Archives Canada/ Sam family fonds/e008441646

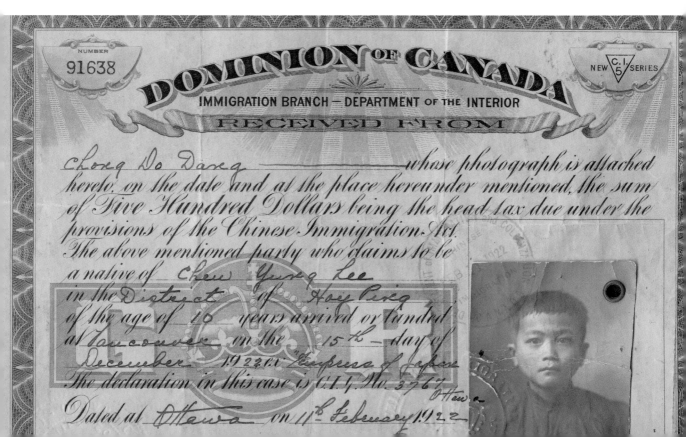

Chinatown in Vancouver, BC.
142220782/Shutterstock.com

house and bought food, clothing and other items from local merchants. In this way, the men who worked overseas in countries like Canada, the United States and Australia helped their home villages grow richer. Some of these villages, like my grandfather's, were able to make municipal improvements, such as installing a water pump and funding a local school for young children.

However, like many Chinese men who traveled to work and live in other countries, he lived through many challenges. In the face of prejudice, it was more important than ever to hold on to the traditions that brought joy to the overseas Chinese and reminded them of their loved ones still in China.

"I could see the whole length of Chinatown stretching east, towards Main Street, a vista dotted with straw hats and vegetable wagons, open stalls, and rows and rows of awnings billowing in the breeze like red and green sails."
—Wayson Choy, author

Chinese New Year Festivals Through the Ages

In the early years of Chinese *emigration*, Chinese New Year celebrations in other countries were often private,

During the Spring Festival in China, people spend their time visiting loved ones and eating lots of good food. However, another activity has become popular recently: going to the movies.

China is the world's second-largest market for movies, right behind the United States. In 2015, people in China spent US$6.68 billion on going to the movies! And the Spring Festival, when everyone has a week off school or work, is one of the most popular times of the year to go to the theater. In 2016, on New Year's Day, people in China spent US$100.5 million on movie tickets, the most they have ever spent in one day.

Two Canadian girls receiving money wrapped in red paper at a Chinese New Year celebration.
Library and Archives Canada/Department of Employment and Immigration fonds/e011044985

organized in homes with friends and family, or in small gatherings at restaurants or clan association buildings. As the communities grew larger, they put on more elaborate festivals. In Vancouver, the first public Chinese New Year celebration occurred in 1959, and the first Chinese New Year parade occurred in 1974. In San Francisco, which has the oldest Chinatown in the world outside of China, the public celebrations began in the 1860s!

While it was important for the Chinese communities in other countries to hold on to their traditions, the New Year parades and festivals were open to other people as well. It was a way for the Chinese immigrants to show the people in their new countries what Chinese culture was about, and also to invite everyone to celebrate together. In countries like the United States, where people were from so many different places, the Chinese community recognized that including everyone in their happiest moments was the best way to make sure that everyone got along. Learning more about other cultures has always been the best way to defeat racism and prejudice. And it looks like

those early immigrants succeeded! In 2016, the Lunar New Year became a legal official holiday in New York State, and was celebrated in Washington, DC, on Capitol Hill for the very first time. Chinese New Year has become a symbol of the strength of Chinese communities around the world and is now truly celebrated by families of all cultures.

Chinese Date Cake

*My sisters and I all agree that this was our favorite Chinese New Year snack. A cross between a pudding and a cake, this date cake, called **nein goh**, was eaten fresh on New Year's Eve and any left over was fried in an egg batter—like French toast—during the rest of the week. Glutinous rice flour is made from a special kind of rice known as glutinous, or sticky, rice. Cane sugar is a type of brown sugar that has been formed into hard cakes that must be broken up or ground before it can be used. All of the ingredients are available at Asian grocery stores.*

Ingredients:

1 cup dried Chinese dates

5¼ cups water
(divided into 3½ cups + 1¾ cups)

⅔ cup cane sugar or brown sugar

1¾ cups potato flour

2½ tablespoons rice flour

1½ tablespoons glutinous rice flour

Sesame seeds

Directions:

1. Place a shallow pan of water in the oven on the lowest rack and preheat oven to 375 degrees,
2. Boil dried dates in 3½ cups of water for 15 minutes. Drain the water from the dates into a medium saucepan. Set the dates aside.
3. Add the sugar to the saucepan and heat the mixture over medium heat until the sugar has dissolved, stirring occasionally.
4. Pour the remaining 1¾ cups of water into a food processor or blender, add the boiled dates and blend until smooth. Press the mixture through a fine-mesh sieve. Discard the solids and reserve the smooth puree.
5. Combine the cane sugar syrup and the date puree. Make sure you have 5¼ cups of liquid; you may have to add more water.
6. Place the flours in a medium bowl, and stir in the liquid until well incorporated. Strain through a fine-mesh sieve and discard any solids.
7. Oil a 9-inch square pan or round pie plate. Pour in the batter.
8. Place in oven on the rack above the steaming pan of water and bake for 15 minutes or until the batter looks firm and you can just see through it.
9. Sprinkle with sesame seeds and let cool completely. Cut the cake into thin slices and serve.

Jen's Story
(Part One)

Jen's grandparents in the 1960s.

Jen Sookfong Lee

Although it was my grandfather who first established our family in Canada, my mother and her mother-in-law, my grandmother, always planned our Chinese New Year celebrations.

In 1956, my grandmother joined my grandfather and my father, who had come to Vancouver in 1951 by himself, as a 13-year-old boy. In those days, Chinatown was still small, and the people who lived there were mostly men who had come to Canada to work before World War II. My grandfather had bought a house and prepared for my grandmother's arrival with winter clothes and as much furniture as he could afford. But it was my grandmother who took on the task of bringing Chinese traditions into their home. And for her, that meant cooking an elaborate meal on New Year's Eve.

It was difficult to find ready-made Chinese food then, so my grandmother made everything from scratch. She started with different kinds of tay: sweet round dumplings filled with creamy red bean paste, crescent-shaped savory dumplings with pork and vegetables, steamed sticky date cake, and cupcakes that looked like open tulips when they cooked.

The eight-course dinner was the star of the show. There were always long cellophane noodles, braised shiitake mushrooms, whole fish, and soup made with bean curd and fat choy. As my grandmother grew older, she taught my mother, her daughter-in-law, to cook these same dishes, which my mother has been doing since my grandmother died in 1980.

My grandmother always insisted that we clean the house before the New Year and wear bright colors like red or pink or purple. She also taught us the traditional sayings that Chinese people use to wish luck on their loved ones.

For my grandmother, and later my mother, keeping these traditions alive meant that they felt closer to the culture they had left. Because they were busy mothers with children and homes to look after, they were not as connected to Chinatown as my grandfather and father were. So, in order to feel like they were still part of a community, and to help their children learn about Chinese culture, they made the New Year a big part of our family life.

For these wives and mothers, coming to a new country and learning about a different culture could be overwhelming, and very few of them had jobs outside the home, so they found a lot of joy in carefully preparing New Year's food and teaching their children the importance of all the different aspects of Chinese New Year.

CNY Facts

While Chinese people today are traveling more than ever, exploration has long been a part of Chinese history. The first ships that could sail across oceans were built in China in the 1200s, and extensive trading with other countries such as India and Kenya began in the 1400s during the Ming dynasty. The man in charge of the imperial fleet of ships was named Zheng He, and he led voyages to Vietnam, Bangladesh and East Africa. His most famous voyage, to Kenya, resulted in a trade: Zheng He offered silk and porcelain in exchange for live giraffes, lions, zebras and ostriches, which he brought back to the imperial court, where the animals were considered to be godly beasts. As you can see, travel and business have always been a part of Chinese history and culture.

Emma's Story

Emma as a child.
Pon Man Lee

In 1978, when Emma Berg, a Vancouver realtor and my sister, was in Grade 4, her teacher broke up her class into groups of three and told each group to create a display that showcased a cultural celebration with which the students were most familiar. Emma's group was assigned Chinese New Year. "Never mind that I was the only Chinese kid in the group—my teammates, Charles and Hiro, were Korean and Japanese. But it didn't matter. We rocked our project," Emma remembers. For their display, the children brought in lucky money envelopes filled with coins, shared deep-fried dumplings and shrimp chips that our mom had made, and performed a dragon dance with a red-and-gold paper dragon they had carefully crafted.

Red envelopes similar to the ones Emma and classmates used in their presentation.
yipengge/iStock.com

A young boy preparing for the lion dance. Usually, boys between the ages of 11 and 16 perform as the heads and bodies of lions during Chinese New Year.

The International Chinese New Year Night Parade in Hong Kong.

BartlomiejMagierowski/shutterstock.com

THREE

HOW CHINESE NEW YEAR IS CELEBRATED TODAY

A Public Holiday

In many Asian countries such as Singapore, Taiwan and, of course, China, Chinese New Year and the Spring Festival are now part of a weeklong holiday. Schools and workplaces in Asia close for one week during Chinese New Year, in the same way they close in other parts of the world during Christmas or Hanukkah. People take the time to rest, visit with their families, travel and eat. Because so many Chinese people live in other countries, away from their families, travel is a huge part of the New Year celebrations.

In many large Asian cities, celebrations are held in public places where lots of people gather. Hong Kong's Chinese New Year festival is one of the most popular

The Hong Kong night parade, one of the biggest New Year celebrations in the world.
coloursinmylife/Shutterstock.com

Chinese New Year fireworks in Hong Kong's Victoria Harbour.
winhorse/iStock.com

"I did not learn about Chinese New Year's until I was 12 years old, and I fantasized about the perfect big warm family gathering that I learned about in Chinese school."
—Frances Kai-Hwa Wang, author

festivals in the world for tourists. The three-day festival begins on New Year's Eve with the Night Parade down Hong Kong's busiest streets, complete with illuminated floats, musicians and stilt walkers. This parade is even shown on television! On New Year's Day, an elaborate fireworks display is set off at the city's Victoria Harbour. And on the third day, people crowd into the Sha Tin Racecourse for an exciting day of horse racing. In recent years, New Year celebrations have included laser light shows, carnivals and rugby matches!

The celebrations for Chinese New Year, like those for any other holiday, change over time to incorporate new technology and ways of thinking. For example, at Christmas, you can now track the progress of Santa Claus with an app on your smartphone. Chinese-language hip-hop musicians perform alongside traditional Chinese opera singers. Parades are live-streamed on the Internet so anyone can watch them, from anywhere in the world. Red lucky money is now sent and received with messaging apps and is called *e-hongbao*. The New Year is about celebrating tradition but is also an opportunity to celebrate the new and exciting things in our lives. While firecrackers pop on the sidewalk, computer-designed fireworks displays bloom overhead.

Family First

At festivals in Asia and around the world, the events are always family friendly. After all, Chinese New Year is all about celebrating family and spending time with our

A family photo being taken on Chinese New Year at Yaowarat Road in Bangkok, Thailand.
Michael Luhrenberg/iStock.com

CNY Facts

Since cash gifts are so much a part of Chinese New Year, trying to meet demand for all that money can be a problem for Chinese banks. Because people make withdrawals to give as lucky red money, the People's Bank of China supplies banks across the country with short-term injections of cash.

Chinese New Year parade in New York City.
a katz/Shutterstock.com

oldest and youngest loved ones. At Chinese New Year parades, the fan dancers, drummers and lion dancers are often children or teenagers. Along the parade route, people marching in the parade or riding on floats pass out candy to the children watching the festivities.

One of the most important aspects of Chinese New Year for children is showing respect and affection to their elders—their parents and grandparents—by visiting and bringing them gifts of fruit, candy and lucky money. This important tradition continues to this day. At a very young age, children are taught Chinese sayings that are meant to wish their elders good luck, long life and good fortune. For instance, Cantonese phrases such as *"Gung hay fat choy"* ("May you have prosperity"), *"Sun tai geen hong"* ("May you have good health") and *"Sun neen fai lok"* ("Happy New

Year") are common in Chinese-speaking families all over the world. Children are expected to engage in the celebrations at home by helping the adults prepare the big dinner and by creating decorations and banners to hang throughout the house. These decorations incorporate paper cut-outs of the coming year's zodiac animal. And older children help adults set off the firecrackers, a noisy and smoky task!

Chinese New Year celebrations, along with many other customs, stick to tradition a lot of the time, with practices like the giving of red lucky money that haven't changed at all over thousands of years. Chinese culture respects progress and invention in business and technology; after all, most of our smartphones are made in Chinese factories. But life at home for many Chinese families often follows traditional customs, like the careful use of color. Lucky days for

Mother and daughter checking their smartphones during a Chinese New Year parade.
Michael Luhrenberg/iStock.com

The Sydney Opera House is lit in red at night to commemorate Chinese New Year.

Banners similar to the ones that are hung in homes and businesses during Chinese New Year are displayed during other celebrations, including birthdays and housewarmings. The only difference is that they're printed or painted with different messages!

money and love are determined by the lunar calendar. **Feng shui**, a way of arranging your home to create harmony and prosperity, is practiced by experts and families alike. The core of Chinese New Year has always been family, and it will remain that way for many years to come.

The Importance of Color

During Chinese New Year, it's common to see red everywhere: red envelopes, red clothing and red candies. Red, however, is an important color in Chinese culture year-round.

Red is associated with fire, with happy and exciting celebrations. This is why you'll see that color on Chinese wedding invitations. Red-dyed eggs are used to celebrate the birth of a new baby. When a new business is established, friends will send potted plants draped in red banners.

Other colors also play a big role in Chinese culture. Gold, the color of wealth and nobility, is also used during Chinese New Year to help welcome in a year of prosperity. Red and gold is a classic combination used in restaurants, Buddhist temples and banks. Chocolate coins wrapped in gold foil are common gifts.

If there is one color that is opposite to red or gold in meaning, it's white. White is traditionally the color of funerals, at which mourners usually wear white from head to toe. White envelopes containing money are given to everyone attending. White is the color of sadness and bad luck, and is never worn or used during celebrations.

"Find something you share, that your cultures share, and use that as a gateway. Use that as a jumping-off point, but don't change yourself so they like you more. They need to appreciate you for who you actually are."
—*Eddie Huang, chef and writer*

Red and gold decorations to celebrate Chinese New Year.
wuviveka/iStock.com

Mother and daughter at a Hong Kong market.
zeynepogan/iStock.com

In Chinese films and television shows, ghosts are often depicted with long white hair and wearing white robes.

It's Not All About the Money

Red lucky money. Gung hay fat choy. Dumplings shaped like gold ingots (oblong blocks of pure metal that can be used to make jewelry or coins). With all these things, it may seem like Chinese New Year is all about money. But if you look closer, *prosperity*, as the Chinese like to call wealth, is about more than just becoming rich.

In traditional Chinese culture, family is very important. When I was a little girl, three generations lived in one house: my grandparents, parents, and my sisters and I all lived under one roof for many years. Our family, like many others, believed that together we were better able to meet everyone's needs, instead of looking to the government or even our friends. In some households, money earned by working is shared by all members and spent on what makes the most sense for the whole family. Mealtimes are often spent together. Decisions about school or work are made jointly by the entire family. And holidays are about eating together and paying respect to the elders.

For most of China's history, ordinary families lived in poverty. Whether they were farmers or fishers, many people struggled to buy enough food or pay the rent on their homes. It was practical to pool resources as a family, and it was important to save money and always look for ways to earn more. Money became a symbol, or something that means more than just the dollars and cents that people earned, spent or saved. Having money meant you could afford to eat. It meant your family wouldn't get evicted from your home. It meant that if someone got sick, you could afford to buy medication. Although many more people have good jobs and earn much higher salaries now in the past, millions of families in China don't earn very much at all, and the struggle to survive continues.

For people who have had difficulty earning enough money to support their loved ones, the Spring Festival is an opportunity to start a new year that could be happier than the one before. And of course, prosperity, or wealth, is an important part of that. The traditions that relate to money are not really about money at all, but about maintaining happiness and health, and keeping your family safe.

CNY Facts

- Twenty percent of the world's population celebrates Chinese New Year.
- In 2014, people in China spent US$100 billion on shopping and eating out during the Chinese New Year period.
- According to China's Ministry of Culture, 119 countries around the world host Chinese New Year celebrations.
- During the Chinese New Year period, 42 million trips are made by air within China.
- In 2013, 500,000 people celebrated Chinese New Year at London's yearly parade through Chinatown and Trafalgar Square.

A Chinese calligrapher and his daughter in People's Park in Chengdu, China.
TkKurikawa/iStock.com

A luxury shopping mall in Shanghai, China, decorated for the Year of the Monkey in 2016.

August_0802/Shutterstock.com

In 2012, over US$74 billion was spent in China on retail items, which include clothing, jewelry and food.

Recently, the emphasis in China has shifted from giving and receiving money during the Spring Festival to buying gifts for loved ones. Many large retail chains from Europe and the United States have opened stores in China in the past few years because people there now have more money to spend on expensive shoes, electronics and other luxury purchases. Gifts can be extravagant, like cakes stuffed with gold ingots, or flower arrangements with money hidden among the stems.

To accommodate this new interest in gifts, shopping malls have been built quickly in the last twenty years and there are now about four thousand across China. The largest mall in the world is in the Chinese city of Dongguan. However, these malls haven't all been successful, and many spaces in them remain empty. New South China Mall was only 10 percent full ten years after it was built and has been called a "ghost mall." This is partly because the malls were being built more quickly than stores could fill them, and partly because the stores that did occupy the spaces were selling luxury, or very expensive, items that people like factory workers couldn't afford. Since then, shops and restaurants that sell lower-priced products and food, have become more common in the malls, and some now include free entertainment areas like the Teletubbies Edutainment Center in the South China Mall.

While Chinese New Year is about survival and new beginnings, it's also big business for stores and restaurants, which are constantly changing to reflect the evolving interests of the Chinese people. And even though money and gifts have a prominent role in the New Year celebrations, the core of what the holiday is really about has always remained the same: the hope that our loved ones will be healthy and happy during the coming year and for many years to come.

"I think that being Asian, you know, having cultural roots, has widened my perspective and helps me to have more compassion for people of different ethnicities and different backgrounds."
—Lisa Ling, journalist

LONGEVITY NOODLES

Long noodles are a part of most traditional Chinese New Year dinners, and families use whatever kind of noodle they like with different sauces and toppings. Some families use chewy wheat or egg noodles, called mein. Some families use rice vermicelli, called fun. They're sometimes fried with meat and vegetables, or included in a soup. In my family, we cooked cellophane or glass noodles (called saifun), which are long and thin and made of mung bean or split pea flour. Raw, these noodles are white and look a lot like vermicelli. Once they're cooked, they're transparent, like glass! My mother prepares them plainly, and we eat them like rice, with other, more complicated dishes spooned on top. All of the ingredients are available at Asian grocery stores. This recipe makes 4 side-dish servings.

Ingredients:

¼ cup dried shrimp

8.8 ounce package of cellophane noodles

½ cup chopped green onion

⅛ cup light soy sauce

1 tablespoon sesame oil

Salt and white pepper to taste

Directions:

1. Soak shrimp in room-temperature water for 10 minutes. Drain water and chop shrimp roughly.
2. Bring a large pot of water to a boil. Drop in the noodles and boil for 4 to 5 minutes, or according to the directions on the package. Drain.
3. Combine shrimp, green onion (reserving some for garnish), soy sauce, sesame oil, salt and pepper with the noodles. Toss until well mixed.
4. Transfer to serving bowl and top with the reserved green onion.

Jen's Story
(Part Two)

Jen's mother and sisters in 2002.

Jen Sookfong Lee

When I was a child, my sisters and I were responsible for helping my mother make the tay, the snacks that our family would eat through the Chinese New Year week. These tay were often dumplings, filled with sweet red bean paste or a savory stir fry of pork and vegetables. Our mother spent days boiling down the red beans with cane sugar and then pressing the mixture through a sieve to make a smooth, buttery paste. And before she owned a food processor, she used two big cleavers to mince the pork and vegetables as finely as possible.

As kids, the part we enjoyed the most was kneading and pressing the dumpling dough. My father made a dough press from two cutting boards connected by a hinge on one side. Our job was to break off a piece of dough and roll it into a ball the size and shape of a table tennis ball, then press it flat between the two sides of the dough press. When we pulled the press apart there was a perfectly round disc of stretchy dough, ready to be filled, folded and pinched shut. My mother would then smooth out any bumps and deep-fry the dumplings until they were crispy and brown. It was a lot like playing with modeling clay, except we got to eat our handiwork afterward!

Now that my sisters and I have children of our own and my mother is a widow in her seventies, our celebrations for Chinese New Year have changed. My mother plans two dinners: one for New Year's Eve and one for New Year's Day. On New Year's Eve, we all gather at my mother's house, where she greets us with a bowl of candy, made up of brands popular with Chinese children, like Sugus, White Rabbit and Frutips, and also brands common in Canada, like Ferrero Rocher and Almond Roca. During Chinese New Year, children can eat as much candy as they want, which my son really enjoys! Then, we help her fry the last of the tay before packing them into small boxes for us to take back to our homes, along with a handful of candy and a mandarin orange with a stem and leaf still attached, to symbolize long life. My sisters and I all help my mother prepare the dinner, while the children play, often with the stuffed toys (usually of the coming year's zodiac animal)

Dumplings.
bhofack2/iStock.com

Lucky money.
Shoutforhumanity/Dreamstime.com

and noisemakers my mother has bought them. My sister Tina sets the table in the way my mother likes it organized, with no dishes placed in straight lines of three (which my mother associates with death) and chopsticks placed perfectly straight. When we finally sit down to eat, we have to be careful not to drop any food or our chopsticks. This can bring bad luck for the year ahead.

The next morning, the children must greet my sisters and me with traditional New Year sayings before receiving their red lucky money. The first thing they eat is even more candy, before breakfast! My mother spends the morning at her Buddhist temple, where she prays for prosperity and peace for all of us. In the evening, we meet at a restaurant for another dinner, but this time there is no work, only relaxation and fun. Similar to Christmas, Chinese New Year's Day for our family is about resting, celebrating and spending time with one another. For many years, we always met at a Chinese restaurant and ate a ten-course meal with traditional New Year dishes, but lately, we have been trying different cuisines, like Korean, Japanese or Vietnamese. In the same way that Chinese New Year has been changing as people move around the world, the celebrations in my family have changed also. After all, three of my mother's six grandchildren are **mixed race**, so it makes sense for the whole family to celebrate in as inclusive a way as possible.

Thean Hou Temple in Malaysia, decorated for Chinese New Year.

WEKWEK/iStock.com

Elaine's Story

Elaine in 2016.
Elaine Chau

When Elaine Chau was growing up, she didn't know very much about all the things you were supposed to do around Chinese New Year. At the Chau household, they didn't necessarily clean the house from top to bottom, or even exchange red envelopes. But they cooked, and cooking is a useful skill for Elaine, who often reports on food and restaurants for programs on CBC Radio. Her mom loves to cook, and ever since Elaine was 6, she would watch her and ask to be her helper.

"I was a bratty kid," Elaine admits, so it was rare that she was willing to be taught anything, and cooking during Chinese New Year became a sort of truce with her mother. Their conversations during the rest of the year consisted of her mom telling her to do something and Elaine yelling or sulking in response. But in the kitchen during Chinese New Year, their language changed. Cooking became their language.

Elaine learned how to fold dumplings and make the most glutinous nein goh. With every dumpling fold and tasting of the cake batter, she was learning more about her mom. She spoke through the making of those dishes. And, in those years of conversations, Elaine finally began to understand her mother. Through food, her mother

Preparing dumplings.
tonisvisuals/iStock.com

was saying, "I feed you and I teach you to feed yourself because I love you."

Now, Elaine laughs and says, "The dynamics of my relationship with my mom have not deviated much since then." Sure, her mother still lectures, and sometimes Elaine still yells. But every Chinese New Year, they let the food they make together remind them of the love they share.

Elaine and her parents in the 1990s.
Elaine Chau

63

Chinese dance with a fan at New Year's in
Johannesburg. These children are from Amitofo
Care Centre, an orphanage based in Lesotho.

CHINESE NEW YEAR CELEBRATIONS ACROSS THE GLOBE

Around the World

People of Chinese descent live outside of China in 130 countries around the world, which is why Chinese New Year is celebrated in so many different cities. Members of my extended family live in Singapore, Australia, and many cities in Canada and the United States. Along with food, the events of the New Year are the most popular and most well-known parts of Chinese culture.

In cities such as San Francisco or Sydney, Australia, where there are lots of people of Chinese descent, there are also many different communities of people from all over the world. Years and years ago, when the first Chinese men

Chinese New Year celebrations in Bangkok, Thailand.
Michael Luhrenberg/iStock.com

Rooster lantern based on the Chinese zodiac, in Sydney, Australia.
lovleah/iStock.com

Giant horse lanterns based on the Chinese zodiac, in Sydney, Australia.
lovleah/iStock.com

to live outside of China began organizing New Year celebrations, they wanted to make sure that everyone, including non-Chinese people, felt comfortable enough to watch and also participate. Now, in Vancouver, when I take my son to watch the New Year parade, a team of Scottish bagpipers and people in traditional First Nations regalia march alongside Chinese fan dancers. In Toronto, Bollywood dancers join in the fun. Even at Disneyland, there are Chinese drummers and a dragon parade, and Mickey and Minnie Mouse dress in traditional Chinese attire.

What makes each celebration unique is how the local cultures have influenced the way people organize and experience the festival events. In Sydney, more than seventy events are included during the Chinese New Year Festival. For two weeks, there are dragon boat races, fashion shows, art exhibits and a lantern festival.

London Eye lit up for Chinese New Year.
Pjgibson/Dreamstime.com

In 2016, the City of Sydney asked twelve artists to create giant lanterns inspired by the Chinese zodiac and placed them in prominent locations, like at the famous Sydney Opera House. This festival was called Lunar Lanterns and even offered guided walking tours to each of the lantern locations. In London, the famous London Eye is lit in red and gold. The New York Philharmonic often plays a special Chinese New Year concert. While some traditional components stay the same—the parade, the lion dancers, the focus on family and food—each community of Chinese people has settled into new countries and taken on new customs and jobs. And the most famous Chinese holiday of all, the New Year, takes on new ways of celebrating to reflect these changes.

"I came to this country as a refugee and I was taken into Canada and I felt I belonged. People sometimes want me to say that I didn't feel I belonged because I was Chinese or I was different, but I didn't ever feel that."
—Adrienne Clarkson, former Governor General of Canada

Twenty percent of the world's population takes part in Chinese New Year in some way, whether that means attending a parade or eating the special tay or watching performers sing and dance late into the night. It seems that the dream of the first Chinese men to settle in other countries has come true: Chinese New Year truly has become a global celebration for everybody.

A Different Kind of Traveler

Since the 1980s, China has grown quickly, and more people are starting businesses and making more money than ever before. For a long time, the people leaving China to live in other countries were fleeing a Communist government that restricted many aspects of their lives, including what they learned in school and what jobs they could hold.

A dancing dragon at a New Year's parade in Jakarta, Indonesia.
Yamtono_Sardi/iStock.com

Chinese New Year celebration in Bangkok, Thailand.
aluxum/iStock.com

- There are 39.5 million Chinese people traveling to find work, all over the world.
- In Europe, the largest community of Chinese people is in the United Kingdom, where 630,000 people of Chinese descent live, mostly in London.
- Following the oil industry, many Chinese workers are now living in several African countries, including South Africa and Tanzania.
- Singapore is the only country besides China that is mostly (77 percent) made up of people of Chinese descent.
- In the first half of the 20th century, most of the Chinese citizens who moved to North America did so to find work or for political reasons. Now, the movement is mostly educational, with Chinese students enrolling in universities and colleges all over the United States and Canada.

Now that China has become a superpower, many families find themselves with spending money for the first time in generations. Chinese people travel to other countries to attend universities and colleges, or are establishing businesses. And they are also traveling for fun. In 2012, 176 million people from China traveled during the Spring Festival to various different countries, including Thailand and Indonesia, where there are many resorts for rest and relaxation.

For cities that are popular with Chinese tourists, it makes sense to include Chinese New Year celebrations during the only time of the year when most Chinese citizens have a week off. In Las Vegas, Nevada, the celebration is called Chinese New Year in the Desert. Casinos and hotels there host lion dances and buffets featuring Asian dishes. At the Forum Shops at Caesars Palace, a hotel and casino in Las Vegas, a twenty-two-foot-long dragon made

Conservatory and botanical gardens at the Bellagio Hotel in Las Vegas, Nevada.
Kobby_dagan/Dreamstime.com

of thirty thousand red and gold LED lights is proudly displayed every year. And famous pop singers from China and Taiwan travel across the world to perform in elaborate Las Vegas–style shows during the festival week.

Even while traveling to relax, it remains important to many Chinese to follow the customs of the New Year and ensure that the coming year is full of health and happiness. The people of China have been moving around the world for thousands of years, and have always celebrated the New Year wherever they are, no matter the circumstances.

The New Diversity

Every year, I take my son to watch the Chinese New Year parade in Vancouver. Like most children, he is excited by the police motorcycles driving in formation and the candy and coins that local politicians and community leaders pass out to spectators lined up along the streets of Chinatown. When the fan dancers appear, he asks me to tell him the story of my best friend, Vicki, who, as a child, performed the fan dance for Prince Charles and Princess Diana of the United Kingdom. And he likes the stories about my cousins Sonny and Tony, who appeared in many Chinese New Year parades when we were teenagers, both as drummers and dancers, performing as the body of one of the lions or as the long, snake-like dragon. As much as my son says he likes the firecrackers, the loud noise does make him cover his ears!

My son is mixed race. He is Chinese from my family, but he is Ukrainian, Swedish, Irish, Scottish, English and Cree from his father's family. This sounds complicated, but my son is typical of many children growing up in Canada

In 2011, 1.5 million people in Canada identified Chinese as their ethnic origin. In 2010, 3.8 million people in the United States identified as Chinese.

Fan dancers in the Chinese New Year parade in Vancouver, BC.
Sergei Bachlakov/Shutterstock.com

Children in the Chinese New Year parade in Vancouver, BC.

"Obviously I don't want to make my career a totally political thing, but I care about young Asian-American girls growing up thinking they can never be the stars of their own stories."
—Constance Wu, actor

and other countries where communities of people from all over the world live. His family is global.

It's important to me and to his father that our son learn about the many different places his family comes from. And this means celebrating different cultural events as much as we can. Chinese New Year is the biggest, most prominent Chinese holiday of the year, and while he will grow up playing hockey, wearing a kilt and eating perogies, he will also learn that the Chinese New Year celebrations are an important part of his and his family's background.

Conservatory and botanical gardens at the Bellagio Hotel in Las Vegas, Nevada.
Kobby Dagan/Shutterstock.com

Stephen's Story

Stephen in 2016.
Stephen Hui

When Stephen Hui was a kid, every time Chinese New Year came around, he couldn't wait to go to Chinatown for the parade. "I loved to watch the lion dancers frantically attack hanging balls of lettuce as firecrackers popped all around them," the Vancouver-based journalist and photographer remembers.

But there was one thing he didn't look forward to come January or February: nein goh, the ever-present Chinese date cake. Like clockwork, Stephen's mom would insist that he, or one of his brothers, bake this New Year's dessert to mark the occasion.

Many people prepare this cake by steaming it in a pot on the stove, as the recipe on page 41 directs. But Stephen's family always baked it in the oven.

"Making nein goh wasn't actually much of a chore," Stephen admits. "It's just that the bland cake we made— browned on the outside, squishy on the inside—wasn't really deserving of that label. Why make the effort when Chinatown bakeries have yummy *gai mei bao* (cocktail buns) and *dan tat* (egg tarts) on offer?"

These days, he attends the Chinese New Year parade to watch the lion dancers as much as he does to observe the

Gordon Campbell, former premier of BC, hands out lucky money at the Vancouver Chinese New Year parade.
nbriam/iStock.com

gangs of politicians handing out red lucky money. "They're hoping good fortune will smile upon them come election time," he jokes.

But no matter what, while Stephen is taking in the festivities, he always remembers the taste of nein goh.

Amanda's Story

Amanda in 1983.
Amanda Growe

Amanda Growe is a Jewish Canadian who's been interested in Chinese and Japanese culture since she was young. Growing up in Vancouver, she had a lot of classmates with Chinese and Japanese backgrounds. Amanda says, "I've always felt more interested in these cultures than in Judaism." Recognizing her interest, her parents often took her to the Chinese New Year parade in Chinatown.

Amanda started celebrating the Lunar New Year Japanese-style when she lived in Japan about fifteen years ago. While there, she began the practice of sending *nengajo*—New Year's cards decorated with a traditional message and things like New Year's imagery, the upcoming year's zodiac animal, a photo of the person or family sending the card, or art created by the sender.

These days in Japan, New Year's Day is celebrated on January 1, rather than according to the lunar calendar. Amanda is now back in Vancouver, where the Lunar New Year is predominantly a Chinese celebration. Canada Post issues Lunar New Year stamps, and if the holiday occurs early enough in a given year, Amanda likes to use them on her nengajo.

"Nengajo," she says, "have been my strongest tie to Japan, enabling me to stay in touch with the people I met there." They're also the holiday cards she sends to friends and relatives across the world, in both English and Japanese. Unlike Christmas cards, they feel comfortable to her as a Jewish person. Amanda also uses them to explain the Lunar New Year to her 5-year-old son. "It is important," she says, "for both our connection to Japanese culture and also to Chinese culture, a big part of life in Vancouver." Amanda likes to remind him that besides being a "rabbit-year person," he was born in April, a time of year associated with bunnies. He also happens to like rabbit stuffed toys.

A sample of nengajo, traditionally given and received at New Year's in Japan. These were made and received by Amanda, who used to live in Japan.
Amanda Growe

すてきな一

昨年中はいろいろとお
ありがとうございました
本年もよろしくお願い申

迎春

お健やかに新年をお迎えのことと思います。相
相変わらず諸々のボランティア活動、藍染や山
孫守等の日々を過ごしております。「塩の道」歩
今年は長野県穂高からです。
　皆様のご健康とご多幸を祈念しております。
本年もよろしくお願い申し上げます。
　平成28年　元旦　　おげんきですか

賀

正

nuary 1, 2011

I wish you a h

本年てよろし

あけましてお

HAPPY NE

今年も素晴らしい一年

Children waiting for their turn in a New Year parade.
Bepsimage/iStock.com

A final word from the author

When I started writing this book, I thought I knew a lot about Chinese New Year. I grew up surrounded by loved ones who always insisted on keeping the celebrations alive. But what I discovered about the early travelers who bravely crossed oceans is that Chinese New Year was their way of bringing Chinese culture to their new homes. They invited new friends, who may not have known anything about China or its traditions, to share in the parades and food, and created a holiday that is celebrated in countries all over the world. To this day, people from China are constantly traveling and are still inviting friends, both old and new, to join in the fun.

To those men and women of the past who organized and established Chinese New Year as a much-loved global celebration, thank you for sharing good wishes and good food with the rest of the world.

A note from the series editor

"The Origins are built on the bedrock of personal stories, enhanced by careful research and illuminated by stunning photographs. No book can be all things to all people, and no two people experience a culture in the same way. The Origins are not meant to be the definitive word on any culture or belief; instead they will lead readers toward a place where differences are acknowledged and knowledge facilitates understanding."

—Sarah N. Harvey

Giant rabbit lanterns based on the Chinese zodiac, in Sydney, Australia.

lovleah/iStock.com

GLOSSARY

calligraphy—a commonly used form of writing with Chinese characters, done with brushes and ink to create decorative images that are often displayed like paintings

cheongsam—a Chinese-style silk dress often embroidered with dragons

Chinese zodiac—an astrological system that follows the lunar calendar to predict horoscopes based on the twelve animal signs of the year.

Confucius—a Chinese philosopher who was born in 551 BCE and whose teachings deeply influenced culture, family and government throughout Asia

dictator—a government leader who doesn't listen to the people or his/her advisors.

emigration—leaving the country you live in to move elsewhere

fat choy—a black moss that is used in Chinese New Year dishes, partly because it sounds like the last two words in the common New Year greeting "Gung hay fat choy"

feng shui—a way of arranging homes, gardens and workplaces to promote harmony and happiness

filial piety—one of the most famous teachings of Confucius that details how the elders in a family are to always be respected, and how the most important unit in society is the family

gung hay fat choy—the most commonly heard greeting during Chinese New Year, which means "May you have prosperity." Sometimes heard with other greetings such as "Sun tai geen hong" ("May you have good health") and "Sun neen fai lok" ("Happy New Year").

head tax—the fee that Chinese immigrants had to pay in 1903 to the government to enter Canada, which, at its peak, was $500, equivalent to two years' salary in China

homophones—words that sound the same but have different meanings. They are very common in the Chinese language, which has only 400 syllables, as compared to more than 15,000 in English.

immigration—entering and permanently moving to a country other than the one you were born in

indentured laborers—workers who agreed to work without pay for years in exchange for the travel costs to a new country, and who were often treated very poorly by their employers

Jade Emperor—a god in popular Chinese mythology who was the ruler of heaven and who also is said to have created and implemented the lunar calendar and Chinese zodiac

lai see—red lucky money traditionally given out at Chinese New Year and other holidays as a wish for prosperity and good fortune. Red lucky money can now be sent and received with messaging apps and is called e-hongbao.

lunar calendar—the traditional calendar used in China, which follows the phases of the moon, with each month beginning with the new moon

Lunar New Year—an alternative name for Chinese New Year, which is often used in countries outside of China such as Korea, Thailand and Vietnam

Mahjong—a popular Chinese game, similar to Western card games such as poker or gin rummy, that uses tiles and involves four players representing the four directions: east, west, north and south

Mao Zedong—the first leader of China's Communist Party, which is still in power today, who defeated the Nationalists after a civil war in 1949. He ruled the country until 1976, under a violent and rigid government.

mixed race—consisting of, representing or combining members of more than one racial group

nein goh—a sticky dessert that is a cross between a cake and pudding, made with glutinous rice flour and Chinese dates, which is commonly served during New Year celebrations

Nián—the mythical beast, whose name is also the Chinese word for "year," who is said to have stalked the peasants of China in the last days of winter, and who was scared away by firecrackers, vivid colours and bright lights, and whose defeat marked the beginning of spring

numerology—the study of numbers, including dates, which some people believe may determine luck or predict the future

pagoda—a tiered tower with multiple eaves, common in Asian countries

potluck—a meal or party to which each of the guests contributes a dish

republic—a country governed by a constitution, a document that describes how the country is to be run and what rights and freedoms citizens have

shrine—a place to worship a particular god or goddess, in Chinese culture often an open-sided red box containing a porcelain figure of the god

Spring Festival—an alternative name for Chinese New Year in China, where the holiday also includes the Lantern Festival, which occurs during the first full moon, usually twelve days after the New Year

tay—sweet and salty snacks, often round or crescent-shaped dumplings, that are served during Chinese New Year

Lanterns hanging in a busy urban alley.
Ekaterina Pokrovsky/Shutterstock.com

RESOURCES

Chapter One

Print:

Casey, Dawn & Anne Wilson (illustrator). *The Great Race: The Story of the Chinese Zodiac*. Cambridge, MA: Barefoot Books, 2006.

Otto, Carolyn. *Celebrate Chinese New Year*. Washington, DC: National Geographic Society, 2009.

Online:

BBC: China: 50 Years of Communism. news.bbc.co.uk/hi/english/static/special_report/1999/09/99/china_50/mao.htm

National Geographic Kids: kids.nationalgeographic.com/explore/countries/china/#china-dragon.jpg

Chapter Two

Print:

Yee, Paul. *Saltwater City: An Illustrated History of the Chinese in Vancouver*. Vancouver: Douglas & McIntyre, 2006.

Yee, Paul, Judy Chan & Shaoli Wang (illustrator). *Chinese Fairy Tale Feasts: A Literary Cookbook*. Vancouver: Tradewind Books, 2014.

Online:

Internet Encyclopedia of Philosophy: Confucius. iep.utm.edu/confuciu

Chapter Three

Print:

Bledsoe, Karen E. *Chinese New Year Crafts*. Berkeley Heights, NJ: Enslow Publishers, 2005.

Online:

Hong Kong Tourism Board: Hong Kong Chinese New Year. discoverhongkong.com/ca
/see-do/events-festivals/highlight-events/chinese-new-year-celebrations.jsp

Chinese New Year—By the Numbers. telegraph.co.uk/news/worldnews/asia/china/12137134
/Chinese-New-Year-By-numbers.html

Chapter Four

Online:

Academy for Cultural Diplomacy: Chinese Diaspora Across the World.
culturaldiplomacy.org/academy/index.php?chinese-diaspora

Chinatown: San Francisco. sanfranciscochinatown.com

City of Sydney: Sydney Chinese New Year Festival.
whatson.cityofsydney.nsw.gov.au/programs/sydney-lunar-festival

INDEX

*Page numbers in **bold** indicate an image; there may also be text related to the same topic on that page*

wuviveka/iStock.com

Acknowledgments

To Ruth Linka and Sarah Harvey, for asking me to write this book and guiding me through a celebratory journey.

To Amanda Growe, Janie Chang, Elaine Chau, Emma Berg and Stephen Hui, who generously contributed stories and photographs.

To Sebastien Merle d'Aubigné, Maya Merle d'Aubigné, Samuel Wesley Donner and Lea Mira Donner, for telling me so enthusiastically what they love about Chinese New Year.

To my mother, for keeping all of the traditions alive for her children and grandchildren.

To my sisters Linda Lee, Pamela Chin, Tina Lee and Emma Berg, for helping me piece together the Chinese New Year celebrations of our childhoods.

To Sarah Ling for being my expert reader.

And, finally, to the Chinese emigrants who traveled fearlessly around the world and brought Chinese New Year with them as a symbol of inclusiveness and joy.

Jen Sookfong Lee was born and raised on Vancouver's East Side, and she now lives with her son in North Burnaby. Her books include The Conjoined, nominated for the International Dublin Literary Award and a finalist for the Ethel Wilson Fiction Prize; *The Better Mother*, a finalist for the City of Vancouver Book Award; *The End of East*; *Gentlemen of the Shade*; and *The Animals of Chinese New Year*. Jen teaches at The Writers' Studio Online with Simon Fraser University, edits fiction for Wolsak & Wynn and co-hosts the literary podcast *Can't Lit*.